POEMS OF A FARMER

by

John Osborne

Volume Three

Introduction

I am in the process of writing my twentieth little book of "Poems of a Farmer", and hope to continue in this vein, but have been requested to produce further compilations of these little books and am therefore including five of the small editions in these new collections: Volume Three containing Editions 10, 11, 12, 1990, 1991. I wish to thank Christine Larden for illustrations, Bridget Rogers for the typing involved and Rita Morgan for her help in furthering the sales of these books when entertaining together.

I wish to extend my deep appreciation to the late John Heddle Nash, The Rt. Rev. Peter Firth, Cynthia Glover, the late Mollie Harris and John Timpson for kindly commending the five editions contained in Vol. 2 and Jeffrey Archer, The Rt. Rev. Nigel McCulloch, Bishop of Wakefield, Sir Harry Secombe, Ken Dodd and Gary Lineker for their similar contributions to the editions contained in Vol. 3.

I dedicate the profits from the sale of these books to Cancer Research/Relief & the Church.

POEMS OF A FARMER
Volume Three
First published, December 1996
First Reprint, November 2000
Published by John Osborne, Lansdown Grange Farm,
Weston, Bath BA1 4DS, England.
Produced and Printed by Newline Commercial Print Ltd, Bath, England.
Typeset by Avonset, Bath, England.

Copyright © John Osborne, 1996, All rights reserved

Contents

The Flower Of Happiness	1
The Flower Of Truth	2
The Flower Of Contentment	3
The Flower Of Tact	4
The Flower Of Wisdom	5
The Flower Of Comfort	6
My Garden	7
Tenants Of Life's Garden	10
Is This You?	11
Accepting Life	14
Darkest Night	16
I Would If I Could And I Can	18
If Only	20
Sadness	22
Loneliness	24
Be Thankful	26
Disappointments	27
Springtime	29
Autumn	30
The Mighty Oak	32
British Food & Farming	34
Thurs Nothin' Vit Ta Eat	36
Thic Stupid Cow	38
When Thic Nurse Catched 'Old A' Me 'And	42
Thic Calf, Them Bees And Tha Vet	44
When I Were Shut In Tha Shed	48

Rubbish	50
Badgers	52
Cricket	54
When Melody Was Born	58
Proper Perspective	60
To Daisy	62
A Tribute	63
The Sky At Night	64
The Past, The Present, The Future	66
When You Marry	68
'Neath A Smile	70
Quiet Times	72
When I Die	74
Kneel Down In Prayer	75
Love Supreme	77
Christmas	79
What Do We Seek?	81

The Flower Of Happiness

There's a flower of Happiness in the Garden of Life
    It's a flower so lovely to see,
      If those who possess it could share it around
      What a wonderful world it would be.

It could change so much for so many
    It could brighten the face that is sad,
      It could help us to see what is good in life
      And not to dwell on the bad.

For it smiles like sunshine through the showers
    Uplifting the weary heart,
      It gives inspiration when all seems lost
      And helps us to make a fresh start.

Yes happiness is but a flower
    Yet everywhere it grows,
      It entirely enriches the atmosphere
      Like the fragrant scent of the rose.

So treasure this flower and help it to grow
    'Till it covers the whole of the earth,
      For it's only then, that we truly shall see
      What this beautiful flower is worth.

The Flower Of Truth

There's a flower of Truth in the Garden of Life
    It's as white as white can be,
    It's a perfect example for us to reflect
    And it's there for us all to see.

Some folk always reflect it
    Whilst others go only halfway,
    You sense they are trying to compromise
    And the white of the bloom turns grey.

It fights many battles in the Garden of life
    For those who truly believe,
    But we must be aware of the weeds growing there
    With no purpose except to deceive.

For sad is the man who when put to the test
    Treads the path of deception,
    For it's twisting and long and sorrow grows there
    Of that there is no exception.

But truth is strong and changes not
    And for it we always must strive,
    For though falsehood at times may seem to succeed
    In the end only truth will survive.

The Flower Of Contentment

There's a Flower of Contentment in the Garden of Life
    A flower for which all of us long,
    It matters not if we're rich or we're poor
    Or whether we're weak or we're strong.

It's a flower that is desperately sought
    By nearly all whom we meet,
    Yet sometimes in striving to find it
    We trample it under our feet.

For it is not found in possessions
    It's a flower of a far different kind,
    And to bloom in its ultimate glory
    The seed must be sown in the mind.

You can tell the people who've found it
    For a certain tranquillity reigns
    And life takes on a new meaning
    Gone are the stresses and strains.

There are many flowers in the Garden of Life
    But to mention only a few,
    There's Patience and Peace, Tolerance and Love
    That can help find Contentment for you.

The Flower Of Tact

There's a flower called Tact in the Garden of Life
    A flower that is greatly desired,
    For there are frequent occasions in life
    When its presence is sorely required.

Some people possess it and put it to use
    Whene'er the occasion requires,
    Whilst other folk lack it and often regret it
    When their tolerance and patience expires.

It is not a flower that is vivid and bright
    Though it stands quite upright and strong
    And its gracious ways can transform many scenes
    As it gently corrects what is wrong.

If all the flowers in the Garden
    Are to bloom to their true potential,
    They need the support of each other
    And the flower of Tact is essential.

So let's try to grow it and keep it
    In the Garden of Life that is ours,
    For we'll all be the richer for having
    Tact as one of our flowers.

The Flower Of Wisdom

There's a flower called Wisdom
    in the Garden of Life which the Master has told us to seek,
    And by listening to Him we may find it
    E'en though we be humble and meek.

For the strong don't always possess it
    It can be grown by the frail and the weak,
    It cannot be purchased or borrowed
    It's a flower that's completely unique.

It needs a soil that's receptive
    Where the forces of good all combine,
    It draws from the roots of experience
    And grows with the passage of time.

It's essential for all in authority
    And in any position of power,
    To humbly strive to grow for themselves
    This priceless and wonderful flower.

It must not be mistaken for knowledge
    For knowledge may not make us wise,
    But if truly we seek it we'll find it
    If we look through the Master's eyes.

The Flower Of Comfort

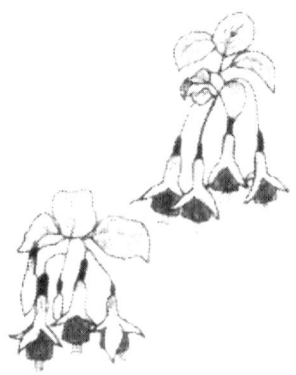

There is a Flower of Comfort in the Garden of Life
    Which all of us long for at times,
    It's so lovely to find a flower such as this
    It embodies exquisite designs.

It radiates warmth when the heart is chilled
    When the soul is an aching void,
    It rekindles the flame of life once more
    When it seems that all's been destroyed.

Like gentle arms it caresses
    Its perfume breathes kindness and love,
    Hope that seemed lost returns once more
    You feel new strength from above.

How often we find in Life's Garden
    Midst all the sunshine and showers,
    A bloom for every occasion
    And comfort is one of those flowers.

My Garden

I love to walk in my garden
    There's so much that one can find there,
    Not just the dew on the roses
    Or the fragrance that's born on the air.

For flowers in their splendour adorn it
    And with their radiant display,
    Transmit to every beholder
    Something that's joyous and gay.

The trees too and the shrubs paint their pictures
    Artistic, majestic, serene,
    And one feels for a moment transported
    As in some heavenly dream.

It's the same whatever the season
    Though we are not always aware,
    For life continues its cycle
    And the wonder always is there.

For peace reigns supreme in my garden
    With seldom a sound to be heard,
    And e'en when the silence is broken
    'Tis oft by the song of a bird.

As I work and walk in my garden
　　I marvel at all that I see,
　　There's a certain grace and a glory
　　Conveying a message to me.

　　For deep in the realms of nature
　　Is the mystery of the divine,
　　And humble I see, and come to accept
　　That the garden is not really mine.

A Thought

If you find someone without a smile
And you do not know the cause,
It may well be the thing to do
Is to give them one of yours.

Tenants Of Life's Garden

We're tenants of Life's Garden
    For nought that we see is ours,
    We're here to enrich and enhance it
    Just as one of the flowers.

The Landlord at all times is present
    He's there to help and to guide,
    To rejoice with us when we are happy
    In sadness to walk by our side.

To assist and share in our problems
    To listen to each single need,
    To give us the strength and the confidence
    In His Name to always succeed.

To help us achieve His ambition
    To walk in the steps He has trod,
    To be always a shining example
    That we truly are children of God.

That we may sow in Life's Garden
    The seeds that one day will be
    The means by which the Glory of God
    Will be there for the whole world to see.

Is This You?

Are you a golden ray of sunshine
    To the folk you meet each day,
    With not just a smile or the way you look
    But with the little things you say?

Does kindness live within your heart
    Do you spread it all around?
    Do you possess these priceless virtues
    Which to-day are seldom found?

The precious things that never change
    The simple and the true,
    The things that really count in life
    Can they be seen in you?

Are you always able to forgive
    When the wounds are really deep?
    Are you at peace with God each night
    Before you go to sleep?

Have you sufficient faith and hope
    When set-backs you receive?
    When faced with grief and sadness
    Do you still believe?

Then hold fast to all these wondrous gifts
    So graciously bestown,
        Remember God Himself has planted them
        By Him the seeds were sown.

Then He will surely bless you
    Fill your days with happy hours
    And e'en when storm clouds gather
    He will guide you through the showers.

A Thought

Never let pride stand in your way
When your heart says you ought to forgive,
For the chance if not taken, may ne'er come again
And you'll regret it as long as you live.

Accepting Life

There are many things we find in life
   That are not easy to accept,
   Some we may anticipate
   And some we least expect.

It may be something personal
   With which we cannot come to terms,
   The loss of someone dear to us
   For whom soul and body yearns.

It may be something less severe
   But still we feel upset,
   The promotion that we tried for
   But found we didn't get.

It may be problems with the business
   When nothing will go right,
   And despite our every effort
   We just cannot see the light.

But we're looking at the dark clouds
   Instead of at the sun,
   And it's folly to accept
   That nothing can be done.

For the blessings that we have in life
    Surround us every day,
    They're countless and continuous
    And can sweep those clouds away.

We have to have the courage
    To ride out all the storms,
    To counter all life's problems
    In all their different forms.

For where there's a will there's a way
    'Tis a truth that overcomes strife,
    We need only to look to the Master
    He's the Way and the Truth and the Life.

Darkest Night

As the sun declines in her golden rays
    And the shades of evening fall,
    We know that soon another night
    Will be upon us all.

To some it will bring welcome rest
    From the toil of a busy day,
    Whilst others view the darkness
    In quite a different way.

It may be through some illness
    Or some problem on the mind,
    When gloom it seems is magnified
    And no answer can we find.

But we must try to realise
    Though it is not in our hands,
    If we always had the sunshine
    'Twould be night in other lands.

There's one thing to remember
    When at times we feel forlorn,
    The dark night will surrender
    To the sunlight of the dawn.

Our Master knew the darkest night
    On the cross at Calvary,
    But His triumphant heavenly light
    Now shines for you and me.

I Would If I Could And I Can

How often we face situations
    And feel we just cannot cope,
    We examine each aspect and angle
    And feel we haven't a hope.

But we really shouldn't look at things
    In this pessimistic way,
    But face each challenge boldly
    with the will to win the day.

For nothing is impossible
    The Master told us so,
    For He has conquered death itself
    So He must surely know.

So when your problems multiply
    This must always be your plan,
    To repeat these words with confidence
    I would if I could and I can.

A Thought

It's wise to pause and consider
Another's point of view,
For the man who's unwilling to listen
Is seldom worth listening to.

If Only

'If' is such a little word
    Which encompasses a lot,
      All those things that might have been
      And those that might have not.

So often in our daily life
    We may pause and think or say,
      If only we'd done this or that
      It might not have been that way.

It is so easy looking back
    To think what might have been
      If we'd known the grass on those distant hills
      Was really not so green.

If we always tried to understand
    And never got upset,
      If we learned the true importance
      To forgive and to forget.

If we had only stopped to listen
    Instead of rushing away,
      We may have helped that person
      Who had something they wanted to say.

If we always showed some kindness
    To every one we met,
    If we always sought to give in life
    And never sought to get.

If only, if only, if only
    We could do a few of these things,
    Then our life could be always reflecting
    The joy and richness it brings.

Sadness

Sadness comes to all of us
   In many different ways,
   Sometimes it only lasts a while
   But at other times it stays.

Perhaps a broken relationship
   And there is no future it seems,
   The whole of your world has fallen apart
   Faded those wonderful dreams.

It could be personal illness
   Or the loss of somebody dear,
   The failure to pass an important exam
   Or something that's much less severe.

Perhaps we feel particularly sad
   When we know we're not understood,
   By those whom we love most dearly
   And our only concern is their good.

Yes! Sadness can strike like lightning
   When we're totally unprepared,
   Or it may creep upon us slowly
   But we know it can always be shared.

For the burden of sadness is lightened
    By friends who understand,
      But the greatest friend is God Himself
    And He offers us His Hand.

Loneliness

There are many battles on the Pathway of Life
    Which we should strive always to win
    But we'll need every atom of strength
    When loneliness comes creeping in.

Clouds of loneliness pass over all
    For some they're just fleeting, then gone,
    But to others they deepen and darken
    And the loneliness still lingers on.

It may be caused by bereavement
    Or perhaps by unthinking friends,
    You feel you just are not wanted
    And no one in the world comprehends.

It comes in many guises and forms
    And can be of our own making,
    If we scorn the comfort of loved ones and friends
    When all is there for the taking.

For there's still much kindness in this world of ours
    As long as we never reject it,
    It can flow like a stream through those lonely hours
    If we're only prepared to accept it.

In fact it may be, if we think on these things
    And we too pass kindnesses on
    In caring and giving we may very well find
    All our feelings of loneliness gone.

Be Thankful

It is so easy for us all
    Each day to fail to see,
      How much we should be grateful for
    And how much in life is free.

The marvel of creation
    The beauty of the earth,
    Do we not consider
    How much all this is worth?

The love of friends and family
    The joy in sight and sound,
    And all the senses we possess
    Are gifts that are profound.

Life itself is our greatest gift
    And God through His dear Son,
    Has made that gift eternal
    To each and everyone.

Yes! There's so much to be thankful for
    Each and every day,
    So in future let's remember it
    When we kneel down to pray.

Disappointments

Disappointments come to all
    Sometime, somewhere, someday,
    But we must just accept them
    As we travel on our way.

Some are only minor
    And soon are brushed aside,
    But some are deep and lasting
    And our sorrow's hard to hide.

They come in many differing forms
    And some are quite expected,
    But some without warning seem cruel and unfair
    And the whole of one's life is affected.

Maybe you feel you've been misunderstood
    By someone who's near and dear,
    The words that you used were spoken in love
    But it seemed they just didn't hear.

Perhaps there is someone you've trusted and loved
    And confided in over the years,
    Who somehow has changed and broken those bonds
    And your eyes still oft fill with tears.

You may feel you haven't achieved much
    You've missed out on so many things,
    But success should not only be counted
    By material gain which it brings.

Your children maybe have not always adhered
    To the things you've endeavoured to teach,
    And you feel in your heart, that in some way you've failed
    There's something you just couldn't reach.

But some of these thoughts may not be correct
    If only the whole truth were known,
    For in God's good time much fruit may be
    Grown from the seeds which are patiently sown.

So when clouds of disappointment
    Dominate the sky,
    We may not understand them
    Or know the reason why.

For life has many sad times
    But also many thrills,
    And if we've walked the valleys
    We'll appreciate the hills.

Yes! Christ knew disappointment
    When His disciples forsook Him and fled,
    But it never matched the Glory
    Of His rising from the dead.

Springtime

As spring breaks forth and breathes new life
    Through natures great domain,
      Flowers paint once more the countryside
      And the trees are dressed again.

We see the transformation
    Of lifeless things reborn,
      A glimpse maybe of God Himself
      As the magic of the dawn.

How wonderful to see such things
    So gentle yet so strong,
      Bulbs breaking through the crusted earth
      Birds bursting forth in song.

It is so marvellous to observe
    The wonder springtime brings,
      For it paints in earthly pictures
      So many heavenly things.

But of all the wonders she reveals
    Perhaps the gem of her collection,
      Is the marvellous way that she portrays
      The glorious resurrection.

Autumn

I love all the seasons
    But if I had to choose but one,
    I think maybe eventually
    It's to autumn I'd succumb.

I love the nip in the morning air
    The colours of the trees,
    The green, the gold, the brown, the red,
    In their varying degrees.

They stand serene in majesty
    A sight beyond compare,
    Until the frosts and autumn winds
    Strip their branches bare.

But even then they're still unique
    As the sun sinks down and sets,
    For they etch themselves against the sky
    In glorious silhouettes.

Then no sooner 'neath those western hills
    Has the golden sun sunk down,
    Than the moon her silver radiance brings
    And claims her heavenly crown.

The fruits of field and garden
    Are once more safely stored,
    And it's wise that we remember
    To always thank the Lord.

Then with harvest all completed
    The cycle starts again,
    The furrows turn, the soil's prepared
    And once more we sow the grain.

You can see why autumn's special
    To one who farms the land,
    For some mysteries of creation
    I begin to understand.

Yet I feel I know so little
    And have so much to learn,
    But God alone can teach me
    How the wheels of nature turn.

So I'm grateful for the seasons
    And the wonders they unfold,
    But when it comes to scenic beauty
    It must be Autumn Gold.

The Mighty Oak

How great thou art thou mighty oak
    Serene and strong you stand,
    Thy branches spread their canopy
    Surveying all the land.

In daylight's glorious sunshine
    Or in night time's lonely hours,
    Countless birds and creatures
    Seek refuge in thy bowers.

We see in every springtime
    The resurrection story told,
    As from thy bare and lifeless branches
    Such wondrous leaves unfold.

Throughout all the summertime
    Their beauty is displayed,
    And when the sun is overpowering
    Their mantle gives us shade.

Then the acorns from thy bounty
    So graciously provide,
    A harvest for the wildlife
    That fills our countryside.

O tree of England still grow on
    Spread thy branches far and wide,
    Of all the trees that grace our land
    Thou art ever England's pride.

British Food & Farming

British Food and Farming
    Has always been the Best,
    The products of our industry
    Have always stood the test.

We take great care in every sphere
    And in our presentation,
    We seek to always satisfy
    And we're proud to serve the nation.

In some fields we are criticised
    For being too productive,
    But the criticism sadly
    Is often not constructive

Some folk won't discuss things
    And are even quite offensive,
    Modern livestock farming
    They say is too intensive.

Most of us would quite agree
    And changes would be nice,
    But could we feed the nations
    And could they pay the price?

Organic farming may be fine
    With no use of any sprays,
    But we can't completely disregard
    All scientific ways.

It is to very difficult
    To keep the balance right,
    For plenty turns to scarcity
    Almost overnight.

For it's not like other industries
    Man is not in control,
    The weather governs harvests
    Right from pole to pole.

It's good maybe that this is so
    It helps us understand,
    That life and growth aren't ours by right
    But gifts of God's good Hand.

Thurs Nothin' Vit Ta Eat

I'm zick a watchin' tha tele
    An' tired a hreadin' tha news,
      'Tis all about vood what we zhouldn't eat
    Wi' cranks just expressin' thur views.

Tha health experts jus' can't decide
    What 'tis we'm gwona get next,
      It may be listeria or p'raps salmonella
    They'm al za blummin' perplexed.

Thur's too much cholesterol zo they da zay
    In milk an' butter an' cheese,
      But our parents di'n't ne'er zeem ta zuffer
    Through 'avin' any a these.

Tha dietitian's zay cut out all vat
    All choc'late, zweets an' red meat,
      But you can 'ave brown bread an' baked beans if ya like
    Or p'raps you prever zhredded wheat.

Yet I da mind 'ow vather zed
    When tha bacon were a little bit vat,
      "Ah! You eat it up wi' plenny a bread
    'Cos there's nothin' a' all wrong wi' that."

Vegetarians can do as tha please
    But I bean't gwon a vollow thur 'abits,
    I respects thur opinions but I can't zee no zense
    In a diet more zuited ta rabbits.

"Animal hrights" be vifty times wus,
    You can't kill a beast ner a bird,
    You must let um increase and let everyone starve
    'Tis all zo blummin' absurd.

Thurs too much zpray on tha tatties
    An' tha water bean't no longer pure,
    Thurs too much pollution an' nitrate
    And things I en't 'eard of bevore.

But 'tis best not ta take any notice
    I jus' don't zee why we should,
    'Cos tha vood what our parents taught us ta eat
    Is tha vood what da still do us good.

Thic Stupid Cow

If you've a kep' cows an' calved 'em
   No doubt zometime you've 'ad,
   A cow what's caused 'e problems
   An' nearly drove 'e mad.

Like tha one what's up an' down all day
   But prevurs ta calve at night,
   An' 'as no intention ta pervorm
   As long as youm in zight.

You leaves 'er vur an hour er two
   An' then goes out again,
   Ta vind that she's still walkin' hround
   An' things be jus' tha zame.

If only she 'ould jus' lie down
   You could check that all were hright,
   But you knows that you'll be lucky
   If you bean't up all night.

But then a hour later
   You vinds that after all,
   She's decided to lie down at last
   But hright agin tha wall.

The veet ur there an' all correct
    but thur's still no 'ope a' all,
    Vur 'er ta calve until she moves
    Or you knocks down tha wall.

You struggles ta get ropes on
    An' are doin' pretty well,
    When up she gets an' hround she goes
    Jus' like a bat in hell.

So you gets a halter
    Ta tie 'er up secure,
    An' you needs a gate to catch 'er
    That's vur blummin' sure.

Ta catch 'er isn't easy
    But you thankvully succeed,
    'Cause yer neighbour's come an' wi' yer zon
    You 'as tha 'elp ya need.

Then you gets ta work agin
    An' tha calvin' all goes well,
    You veels relieved an' thankvul
    You've a damn good calf ta zell.

But you 'aven't vinished yet
    Though tha calf's alive an' strong,
    Tha cow is daft an' walks away
    As though 'e don't belong.

You rubs 'im down an' gets 'im up
    An' trys ta let 'im suck,
    But will she stand, not likely,
    'Tis just your blummin' luck.

You rubs 'er tail an' talks to 'er
    Goes hround an' hround tha shed,
    And when at last 'e gets a teat
    She kicks 'im tha 'ead.

You decides ta tie 'er up agin
    Though yer patience 'as nearly expired,
    'Cause 'tis almost three in tha mornin',
    An' you knows damn well that youm tired.

You must milk out enough vur a bottle
    Ta make sure that tha calf 'as a veed,
    Then you'll try agin in tha mornin'
    An' by then you hopes ta succeed.

Bit I s'pose we should really be thankvul
    Vur both mother an' calf be alive,
    An' though tha cow at tha moment be stupid
    It zeems tha calf 'll zurvive.

Most calvings bean't 'all sa traumatic
    An' oft go accordin' ta plan,
    Vur creation's a marvellous miracle
    Surpassing tha knowledge a' man.

A Thought

The sun shines somewhere everyday
This we know is true,
But if clouds sometimes obscure it
Let it shine through you.

When Thic Nurse Catched 'Old A' Me 'And

I 'ad zum warts come on me 'ands
   I got 'em off a cow,
   I thought mezelve I'll get rid a' they
   But I'm danmed if I know 'ow.

Then zomeone zed, "Tha doctor
   Will zoon get rid a' them",
   'E'll treat 'em wi' zum special stuff
   An' they 'on't come back again.

Well tha doctor passed I to tha nurse
   An' zed, "She'll treat them warts",
   But when thic nurse catched 'old me 'and
   She muddled up me thoughts.

Well I velt quite excited like
   Zittin' there wi' she,
   Then she got a darn gurt thermus vlask
   I zed, "Ah! I'd like a cup a' tea".

But I weredn't quite sa lucky
   'Cus tweredn't tea in thic gurt vlask
   In vact I don't know what it were
   An' I di'n' 'ave time ta ask.

'Cus she dipped a swab stick in thic vlask
    An' dapped em on a wart,
      I could a' kicked thic nurse on both 'er shins
      But I really bean't thic sort.

I thought, "I'll grin an' bear it
    If 'tis gonna do me good",
      An' as long as she did 'old me 'and
      I knew darn well I could.

But she kept on wi' thic little swab
    On all tha warts I 'ad,
      She zed, "I've nearly finished",
      I zed, "Bean't i blummin' glad".

'Cuz tha tears did trickle down me cheek
    An' tha sweat did cover me brow,
      I zed, "I don't think I'd a' bothered ta come
      If I'd a knowed what I know now".

She zed, "'Twill be better tomorrow
    But I shall want ta zee 'e again".
      I zed, "My dear, if they 'a'n't gone now
      Then them warts are gonna remain".

At least it were quite an experience
    If you da unnerstan,
      An' though it were painful, I liked it
      When thic nurse catched 'old a' me 'and.

Thic Calf, Them Bees And Tha Vet

'Ere's zummat what 'appened down on tha varm
    Zummat I'll never vurget,
    I were involved but it chiefly concerned
    A calf, zum bees an' me vet.

Tha story goes zummat like this,
    An' 'tis true what I telle a' course,
    Tha reason tha vet were down on tha varm
    'E'd come ta look at a 'orse.

Well, 'e dressed tha cut on tha 'orses leg
    An' were jus' gettin' into 'is car,
    When I zed, "Now youm 'ere jus' look at thic calf
    'E's up in tha paddock, bain't var."

Zee thic calf 'ad broken 'is leg
    A couple of wiks avore,
    An' tha vet 'ad put un in plaster
    But 'twere rubblin' a little bit zore.

Now tha zun were beltin' down like a vire
    An' 'twere jus' what I were avraid,
    Thic calf weren't nowhere a'tall ta be voud
    'Cuz 'e'd gone off ta lie in tha shade.

We walked all round thic paddock
    Thur weren't ne'r zight nur zound,
    His mother were there but din't zeem ta care
    Zo I knawed 'e wur zumwhere around.

Then I spotted a 'ole in tha 'edge
    Between a couple a' trees,
    I thought mezelve, "If 'e's through there
    'E's behind them 'ives a'bees."

Well sure enough there 'e were
    In tha shade behind a 'ive,
    I thought, you'm stayin' there me zun
    Or I shan't get out alive."

But tha vet zed, "don't 'e worry
    I don't think tha bees 'ull 'urt",
    I zed, "You carry on, I'm stayin' 'ere
    I don't wan' um down me shirt."

'E jus' bent down to touch thic calf
    When tha bees came out be tha score,
    Then 'e waved 'is 'ands and jumped about
    An' out come ten thousand more.

'E zed, "Don't 'e worry, they'm jus' like vlies
    I think they'll zoon be gone ,"
    I zed, "Thic vlie what pitched on I
    'Ad a vootball jersey on."

It weren't very long 'fore 'e changed 'is mind
    An' started ta run an' ta cus,
    I'd already gone 'cuz I knawed in me mind
    That they weren't very vriendly ta us.

They stung 'im on 'is 'and an' neck
    An' got all is 'air in a knot,
    Then one called on I but moved un on quick
    'Cus 'is veet were too blummin' 'ot.

At last we both got back to tha varm
    Veelin' much tha wuss vur wear
    Well, tha vet did look like a golliwog
    Where 'ed vought wi' tha bees in 'is 'air.

Zum things at tha time da zeem vunny
    Yet later you zeems ta vurget,
    But if thurs zummat I'll always remember
    'Tis thic calf, them bees an' tha vet.

A Thought

Many things are a waste of time
But one thing that is surely worthwhile,
Is the joy that you bring to the people you meet
When you wear a beautiful smile.

When I Were Shut In Tha Shed

We 'ad a cow calve tother mornin'
    Tain't usually no trouble a tall,
    But she were a wik er two early
    An' tha calf were a little bit small.

We put 'er in a shed on 'er own
    Cos we knawed she'd need zum attention
    But what transpired from thik little move
    I still 'ardly veels able ta mention.

I jus' wen' in ta give 'er zum cake
    An' to zee whether tha calf 'ould zuck,
    When me zon wen' by an bolted tha door
    'Twere jus' me blummin' bad luck.

I 'eard un drive off on tha tractor
    Ta give me neighbour a 'and
    An' I knawed vrom thik moment 'twere 'opeless
    To do all tha jobs I 'ad planned.

Yer I were, shut in thik shed,
    'Twere all sa blinkin' absurd,
    I coo-eed and called vur all I were worth
    But I'm damned if anyone 'eard.

I thought I'd climb out tha window
    But I couldn't even climb up tha wall
    An' tha honly window I were able ta reach
    Were about a voot too small.

Tha trouble was, it weren't very nice
    Cos thik cow were a little bit quick,
    She kep' blowin' 'er nose an' shakin' 'er 'ead
    An' she knawed I ain't got a stick.

Every time that I 'ad a go
    Ta climb up thik blinkin' wall,
    I did veel 'er 'ead up behind I
    An' I didn't like thik veelin' a tall.

It zeemed like hours I were shut in thik shed
    Wi' no chance a tall ta get out,
    When at last I 'eard tha tractor come back
    An' once more I started ta shout.

At last me zon come back in tha yard
    An' straightway unbolted tha door,
    He laughed vit ta bust, tha more that I cussed
    Well 'e laughed till 'e coun't laugh no more.

But I shan't vurget tha time that I spent
    Shut up in thik shed wi thik cow,
    But I bet a pound 'twon't 'appen again
    I'm damn well telling 'e now.

Rubbish

Tis vunny 'ow zumtimes I zits down ta write
    An' me mind da go blank as can be,
    An' tha more I da try tha wus I da get
    An' this poem is proof as ya zee.

Vor this is a poem what ain't any good
    I can't think why I bothered ta write it,
    I know that 'tis daft, an' I veels blummin' zoft
    Whenever I trys ta recite it.

I don't even know what it's about
    It's just rubbish as var as I see,
    I've read tha damn thing about vifty vour times
    An' it still don't make zense, not ta me.

I can't think why I wrote all these verses
    Da zeem such a darn waste a' time,
    But tis no good vur I ta blame anyone else
    'Cause tha idea in the vust place was mine.

All I can zay is, l'm zorry,
    If only I'd knawed it before,
    I'd a' stopped as zoon as I'd done tha vust line
    But at least I han't written no more.

A Thought

A Wise man said one day to me,
"Be sure you understand,
When you need help, if you have faith
God will take your hand."

Badgers

Now I'm gwoin' ta tell 'e zummat now
   What you 'ardly will believe,
     But I promise 'tis true, 'cause you knows very well
     I bean't tha zort ta deceive.

'Tis tha damage I've 'ad in me garden
   Especially me peas an' me beans,
     'Cause tha badgers 'ave been on tha rampage
     An' destroyed 'em by various means.

They've rolled 'em down, znapped 'em off
   An' eaten all tha pods,
     An' if you da think they'm pretty
     I could shoot tha little s .... blighters!

An' they'm diggin' up me daffidils
   All along tha drive,
     An' I knows that once they've started
     Nothin' will zurvive.

We've broken tha shaft on tha tedder
   An' tipped a trailer up too,
     Just drew droppin' in badger 'oles
     You just can't believe what they do.

We 'ad a cow break 'er leg
    Down a badger's zet,
    An' when things like that da 'appen
    Tain't easy ta vurget.

It ain't just me what's complainin'
    'Tis all me neighbours too,
    'Cause they've zuffered damage in just that zame way
    An' don't know a bit what to do.

'Cause they looks pretty on tha tele
    Wi' a white blaze down their vace,
    You bean't allowed ta touch 'em
    An' I calls it a disgrace.

It zeems zum volk da talk too much
    What just don't unnerstand,
    But they might change their minds a bit
    If they were livin' on tha land.

Vor there's no vear a' badgers becomin' extinct
    I jus' don't zee 'ow they can, 'Cause there's thousands a' zets all over tha place
    An' their only preditor's man.

An' we country volk bean't all stupid
    An' we'm conscious too, don't ya zee,
    Ta kip things in their proper perspective
    'Cause that's 'ow it all ought ta be.

I don't think I'm callous an' I know I'm not cruel
    An' one thing I remembers at least,
    Tha Good Book zez man shall always have
    Dominion o'er tha beast.

Cricket

Tha vust time I played cricket
    I were all convused an' perplexed,
    I didn' know a bit what were 'appenin'
    Nor what I 'ad ta do next.

Tha captain zed, "Vield in tha covers",
    But I coun't vind no cover at all,
    Thur were only one tree down in tha 'edge
    An' thik tree weren't very tall.

We'd only bowled a couple of balls
    When tha batsmen crossed vur a run
    Then tha captain decided ta change us around
    An' I 'ad ta come out in tha zun.

'E zed, "I wants a vine short leg
    I think that you will do."
    I zed, "I don't think I will, 'cause me legs baint that vine
    An' theym long, 'cause, I stands zix voot two."

Then 'e put I in tha slips
    'Twere too darn close vur me,
    Tha vust ball what tha batsman 'it
    Cracked I below tha knee.

I never zid thik ball at all
    'E come za blummin' quick,
    I wish I'd 'ad me wellies on
    Cos me trousers weren't that thick.

When auld Fred bowled agin
    'E shouted out, "Ows zat?"
    I zed, "Main painful I should think"
    Cos 'e missed it wi' 'is bat.

Caught 'n right up on tha thigh
    'Twere a dull like thuddin' zound
    It must a 'urt cos made 'un squeal
    An' roll about tha ground.

Tha humpire zed 'e werdn't out
    But 'e were down a vair aul time
    I never 'eard tha humpire count
    So p'raps 'e were up at nine.

Tha next ball 'it 'is middle stump
    'It un right down flat,
    Zo this time there werdn't any doubt
    'E were out, an' that were that.

An' zo it wernt on vur 'ours an' 'ours
    'Ow I stuck it I never shall know,
    I did bide an' chase thik stupid ball
    Till me legs just 'oudn't go.

Then at last they all were out
    An' we 'ad a cup a tea,
    But tha zun went in an' tha clouds came up
    Black as black could be.

Our vust two batsmen both were out
    An' never zid tha ball,
    In vact we 'ad vive wickets down
    Wi' out a run at all.

Then at last 'twere my turn
    Ta swing thik little bat,
    I thought meselve, "I'll 'it thik ball
    Or I'll eat me blummin' 'at."

I were 'allway ta tha wicket
    When it emptied down wi' rain,
    Zo I never 'it thik little ball
    An' I never played again.

A Thought

When thinking and talking of others
Be careful what is expressed,
Remember to think and talk kindly
For love thinks only the best.

When Melody Was Born

'Twas a soft quiet night in early June
   Two hours before the dawn,
   When Music had her second foal
   And little Melody was born.

A Palomino filly
   With markings quite superb,
   We gazed with joy and wonder
   Yet uttered not a word.

We all just stood there motionless
   'Twas a moment of treasured worth,
   For mares are quick and secretive
   Whenever they give birth.

Soon the gangling legs were striving
   To achieve some sort of stance,
   But with no co-ordination
   They just didn't have a chance.

But with continued perseverence
   They did at last succeed,
   Olympic Melody stood proud
   And looked for her first feed.

It wasn't long before
    Her efforts were rewarded,
    Mother Nature played her part
    And that first feed was recorded.

Next morning everything was fine
    With mother proudly neighing,
    Though I cannot speak the language
    I know what she was saying.

It was truly a lovely picture
    That Music and Melody made,
    For creation was personified
    And its wonder all displayed.

Proper Perspective

It seems to me as a country chap
    That the experts aren't always right,
    They frighten us all with things that they say
    Spreading doom and gloom with delight.

The health experts are some of the worst
    And they keep on changing their mind,
    What was likely to kill us a year or two back
    They now recommend you will find.

Look at the folk who no longer drink milk
    Through listening to some silly fool,
    Yet we had to drink a bottle a day
    When we were children at school.

First there was too much cholesterol
    Now it might not be enough,
    We're finding we're lacking in calcium
    And our bones are not nearly as tough.

Potatoes were bad but now they are good
    Brown bread they aren't quite so sure,
    White sugar they say, is now quite O.K.
    But the water is not always pure.

We've had salmonella to scare us
    Listeria and dangers from lead,
    And now B.S.E., it just seems to me
    That most of us ought to be dead.

The truth is the press and the telly
    Just magnify all that is bad,
    It's blown up, all out of proportion
    And somehow it makes me so sad.

It does so much harm to the country
    And puts fear where no fear should be,
    In their effort to create sensation
    The picture's not true that we see.

It's a pity they can't say something good
    Or find something worthy of praise,
    Instead of finding fault with so much
    And condemning our methods and ways.

For we only need to just look around
    To see how lucky we are,
    We might get things in their proper perspective
    And we'd be the better by far.

We know that its wise to be careful
    And make sure that standards don't fall,
    But let's use commonsense and be thankful
    'twill be for the good of us all.

To Daisy

I know a dear old lady
   Full of charm and grace,
   And when she smiles each wrinkle
   Adds beauty to her face.

She's brilliant with a needle
   And at crochet she excels,
   All her intricate achievements
   A depth of patience spells.

She wears a twinkle in her eye
   And is always full of fun,
   A shining bright example
   To each and everyone.

May she be blest with still more years
   And more ambitions still achieve
   And the golden tapestry of life
   May she with love still weave.

A Tribute

Harold Bowden has just achieved
    Seventy years in the choir,
        Something of which he's a right to be proud
        Something for all to admire.

I've stood beside him many a time
    And with him it was always the case,
        Of attention to diction and richness of tone
        In producing that resonant bass.

He has set standards few can attain
    Walked paths infrequently trod,
        Sincerity lives in all that he sings
        And it's all to the Glory of God.

Yes! What an example he's always been
    And is still I'm thankful to say,
        For the choir of All Saints owes much to him
        Though he never would see it that way.

Those who've been privileged to know him
    Are thankful and proudly rejoice,
        For he's reached this wonderful milestone
        And he still has a beautiful voice.

The Sky At Night

How varied are the pictures
   The sky at night can paint,
   Some awesome, some majestic,
   Some simple and some quaint.

Sometimes in angry billows
   As the waves on a raging sea,
   The dark black clouds seem to speak
   Of that night on Calvary.

Yet sometimes just like cotton wool
   Clouds race across the skies
   And the wonder of the firmament
   Takes on another guise.

Then again all is changed
   The silver moon shines bright,
   The Peace of God personified
   In the silence of the night.

Yes, the moon in all her glory
   Gazes gently down,
   Stars radiantly adorn her
   As diamonds in a crown.

It's then I gaze and marvel
    At those wondrous realms above,
    One senses God's omnipotence
    And His everlasting love.

The Past, The Present, The Future

Look not back upon the Past
    If it should give you pain,
    But be not afraid to learn from it
    For there's much that you may gain.

Those who've gone before us
    Have often taught us much,
    How to cope with tribulation
    When life is filled with such.

There are lives of dedication
    Of sacrificial love,
    Which can give us inspiration
    As strength from heaven above.

So look unto the future
    And step out with a smile,
    For if we're pessimistic
    Each yard becomes a mile.

Yes! Sometimes we'll walk in the valleys
    And sometimes there'll be mountains to climb,
    But all is a part of the jigsaw
    That fashions your life and mine.

For we do not know the pattern
    Life's tapestry may weave,
    But the Master's there to guide us
    Provided we believe.

When You Marry

Marriage is a partnership
    And depends on many things,
    When unity and love prevail
    Much happiness it brings.

It really is quite difficult
    To properly express,
    All we truly wish you
    In terms of happiness.

A perfect understanding
    Of how to give and take,
    A selfless full commitment
    That your vows you'll never break.

A sense of humour, the power to laugh
    The will to win the day,
    For the sun can't always light your path
    And clouds will pass your way.

May you be stronger for their passing
    And grow closer every day,
    Enriched by sharing problems
    As you travel life's highway.

Be thankful for the little things
    The smile, the gentle touch,
    Say each day "I love you"
    It can mean so very much.

May kindness live within your hearts
    May you spread it all around,
    May you see those priceless virtues
    Which today are seldom found.

The precious things which never change
    The simple and the true,
    The things that really count in life
    May they be found in you.

May you always be forgiving
    And turn the other cheek,
    And remember, only he whose strong
    Is able to be meek.

May envy and self pity
    Have no place within your lives,
    But may you culture all things
    Where perfect love survives.

May you have faith and hope and love
    And seek always to believe,
    That he who truly gives in life
    Truly will receive.

May you oft with joy, this day recall
    And retrace the steps you've trod,
    May that Joy be always yours
    And may you Always walk with God.

'Neath A Smile

It's lovely to meet in the course of the day
    A person who's wearing a smile,
      For somehow you too feel uplifted
      And it brightens your day for a while.

Sometimes the smile is so happy
    It needs no words to convey,
      That tinged with laughter and mischief
      The heart is just carefree and gay.

But sometimes sadness is born 'neath a smile
    That brave folk try to conceal,
      And though their smile may benefit us
      We know not how deeply they feel.

For many sorrows are secretly born
    Behind bright and twinkling eyes,
      And the smiling face that's a tonic to us
      Is but a simple disguise.

So no matter how hard life's pathway may seem
    When every step seems a mile,
      Let's hold our heads high and seek always to try
      To face every day 'Neath a Smile.

A Thought

He who's contented with little
Sails life's ocean with ease,
But the voyage can be rough and tempestuous
For the man whom you never can please.

Quiet Times

A quiet time's essential
   For all of us each day,
     A time to pause and ponder
     A time for us to pray.

To recoil for a moment
   From the pace of life, and see
   How oft the picture changes
   When we find tranquility.

Problems unsurmountable
   We find may now be solved,
   Things which seemed so intricate
   Become much less involved.

Our Lord would often take Himself
   Away from all the crowd,
   For the Still Small Voice is stronger
   Than the voice that's always loud.

In the quiet of the hills
   There is so much to be found,
   For nature speaks in many tongues
   And her teachings are profound.

So try to seek some quiet times
    Each and every day,
    It may be that the Master
    Has some special thing to say.

When I Die

Do not be sad or grieve for me
    When my days on earth are done,
    Do not despair, hold on to faith
    For life must carry on.

You will never fear the future
    If you let God take your hand,
    He's been through all life's hardships
    And will help you understand.

Talk to me as you've always done
    And always wear a smile,
    I'll be listening, I'll be waiting
    Parting is but for a while

Think of all the happy times
    And those still yet to come,
    For joy is everlasting
    When God's will is done.

Kneel Down In Prayer

If you're feeling low and your world's upside down
    And no one at all seems to care,
      The best way to find true peace of mind
    Is to simply kneel down in prayer.

For you're never alone in this world of ours
    Though unseen the Master is there,
      And you'll feel His presence and the power of His love
    Each time that you kneel down in prayer.

Though His glorious face He hideth'
    Your burdens He's willing to share,
      And you'll find Him in unlikely places
    Whenever you kneel down in prayer.

He's there in the soul of creation
    Though alas we're not always aware,
      But He speaks in many a language
    In order to answer a prayer.

But the language He uses is always
    A language that everyone knows,
      He may speak through a glorious sunset
    Or the scent of a beautiful rose.

Yes! If with all our hearts we seek Him
   We shall find Him waiting there,
And gently His arms will enfold us
   If only we kneel down in prayer.

Love Supreme

It is not always easy
    To turn the other cheek,
    It takes tremendous courage
    And the world may think you weak.

When loved ones seem against you
    And cause your heart to bleed,
    It's harder still to contemplate
    How love can still succeed.

How hard it is to do your best
    When it's not appreciated,
    How hard it is to still love on
    When it's not reciprocated.

How difficult it often is
    Midst the toil of a busy day
    To give some time to a soul in need
    And some act of love display.

The 'Get well' card, the phone call,
    The visit or the flowers
    Can express a loving thought,
    The choice is simply ours.

We all can make excuses
    But no matter what we say,
    We know that if the will is there
    Love will find a way.

For love knows no dimensions
    And never claims reward
    But reflects when given freely
    The Commandment of our Lord.

He also tells us clearly
    It is there for us all to see,
    "Inasmuch as ye did it unto the least of these
    Ye did it unto Me."

So let's make every effort
    To fulfil this golden dream
    To make this world a better place
    Where Love can rule supreme.

Christmas

All of us love Christmas
   And it's only right that we should,
   For it's a time for caring and giving
   And for all that it is noble and good.

A time to break down the barriers
   That keep people and nations apart,
   A time to convey a message of love
   A time to make a fresh start.

For it really is sad when we pause and reflect
   How we all have wandered away,
   From that real message and meaning
   That came on that first Christmas Day.

A child in a lowly stable born
   So humble and gentle was He,
   The Son of God incarnate
   And He came for you and for me.

To show by his own example
   How we should fashion our lives,
   To prove to us, when all seems lost,
   That perfect love survives.

So let us all remember
    In this time of festive cheer,
    To seek to spread its message
    Throughout the coming year.

Yes! When the Christmas season's over
    And our celebrating done,
    May we thank God with all our hearts
    For giving us His Son.

What Do We Seek?

As we approach another year
   And ponder what's in store,
   Will we find the journey hard
   On paths not walked before?

Will we step with apprehension
   As we journey on our way,
   Or will we walk with confidence
   With the will to win the day?

All of us are different
   Yet, in some ways we're the same
   And many principles in life
   Forever will remain.

Let's consider for a moment
   Our most important quest
   And make certain that for everyone
   We are seeking what is best.

For the paths we take can doubtless
   Other folk affect,
   Leaving deep impressions
   In ways we least expect.

So let's be grateful for each dawn
    And each day seek and try
    To do some deed of kindness
    Lest the chance should pass us by.

May we always be forgiving
    And turn the other cheek
    And remember only he who's strong
    Is able to be meek.

May we spread some happiness
    And wear a twinkle in our eye,
    It's a tonic that costs nothing
    And is surely worth a try.

Let envy and self-pity
    Have no place within our lives,
    But let us culture all those things
    Where perfect love survives.

Instead of asking more of life
    Let's be content to serve,
    For if we count our blessings
    They are more than we deserve.

May we have faith and hope and love
    And seek always to believe
    That he who truly gives in life
    Truly will receive.

For he who's wise is humble
    And in some way understands
    That God can give us all things
    He has the whole world in His hands.